Imaginary Logic

Imaginary
Logic

poems

Rodney Jones

Houghton Mifflin Harcourt
Boston   New York   2011

For information about permission to reproduce selections from this book,
write to Permissions, Houghton Mifflin Harcourt Publishing Company,
215 Park Avenue South, New York, New York 10003.
www.hmhbooks.com

Library of Congress Cataloging-in-Publication Data
Jones, Rodney, date.
Imaginary logic : poems / Rodney Jones.
   p. cm.
Includes bibliographical references.
ISBN 978-0-547-47978-1
I. Title.
PS3560.O5263I43 2011
811'.54—dc22   2010049829

Book design by Greta D. Sibley

Printed in the United States of America

DOC 10 9 8 7 6 5 4 3 2 1

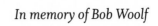

In memory of Bob Woolf

Who knoweth the spirit of man that goeth upward and the spirit of the beast that goeth downward to the earth?

— Ecclesiastes 3:21

Contents

IMAGINARY LOGIC

In the Days of Magical Realism

I went everywhere with invisible
camera crew and musicians.
Portaged by lust, convinced it was beauty.

Washington, early spring, 1976,
three girls moving away from the cab,
speaking French, as I crawled in,

and one, faux-blond, with pearls,
decked out in hotpants and shawl —

I saw her as a zoologist sees a pet
detransmogrifying from a carpet

and was wondering might this ideal
suggest goddess, hooker, or model

when the look she threw back over one shoulder
rendered into stone the eyes
with which I had seen myself.

Voice Making the Sounds of Engines

Aging imaginary playmates,
arbiters of loneliness
and childhood, have they
fallen on hard times,
sleeping under bridges
and eating from trash bins?

When I knew them,
they already had wives,
experience in the military,
and full-time jobs:
mechanic, truck driver,
steam shovel engineer.

In the shadows under
the house of women,
they used to help me
with heavy equipment,
laying out boulevards
for a city of missing men.

Idols, stooges, parrot
and laminate of *vox*
mundi, backfiring, double-
clutching, from this distance
they seem stalled
in the fifties and leaking grease.

Except for the clean,
well-spoken one,
twisting his mustache
like an appellate judge
or ambassador from
the commonwealth of mothers.

And the rooster Caesar,
worm-poaching with
harem and sycophants.
Vuden, vuden, we would go,
and he would show us
the nature of masculinity.

Ambition

The new house had the air
of a stationary ark
ready to set out: the flood
a freshet in each faucet,

the shine and lacquer smell,
pecan floors, transfigurations
of porcelain and enamel.
Each plug-in was an owl's face

being attacked by a snake.
The fear that he might slip
and flush down the toilet
balanced his wishing

the Apaches could leap
from the television. Meanwhile,
since the carpenters
had left a few light boards

stacked by the door, he plundered
the vacant house in the field
for wings, six years old
with an airplane to build.

On Fiction

To enjoy a story I have to put myself in the protagonist's shoes —
     literally — as if
for the instant of the telling, I have become the ideal podiatrist,
     and I expect
real scenes — a stable at a hunt club or a Kwik Mart by an overpass —
and actual people with cowlicks or neck braces, even if they
     shortly will defy gravity
or experience multiple orgasms of such proportions as to wipe out
     audits and biopsies.
I want, too, an account of useless virtues, and eccentrics —
     perhaps
a hermit amnesiac with an altruistic streak or a senator who knits.
Tension goes without saying, a fact like temperament,
     politics, or humidity,
which people die from every day, but that usually must avoid
     direct telling
else we have on our hands a prospectus, dissertation, or treatise.
     Not a story in an event.
A story needs description and dialogue, those mutually parasitic
     engines of attention.
Given language, the story tells itself. But take language back,
you have the loneliness of the author, a quantity one must depart
     in the middle of the night
and travel from tentatively by a series of unanticipated detours
     through a whiteout blizzard.
One friend wore a stocking over his head, seated in his basement
     like a mad
stock-car driver with a yellow sheet rolling onto the platen
     (it had to be yellow)

of an old manual Underwood. Sweating the generative sound,
    he left commas for later drafts.
Another wrote at Denny's on a legal pad (white not yellow). He liked
    having
around him the companionable irrelevant chatter. He wanted
    to live in the world
not out of it, and also to attain the feeling the extraordinary person
    most relishes:
to know unexceptional people with names like Betty or Dot,
    who still need
stories and will tell them without saying a word — a few people,
    professors mainly,
claim that the story has died, but most people, if they listen,
    know that, in order
for the story to die with any significant style, time must stop passing.

The Competition of Prayers

Blessings go fastest, then benedictions,
and harvest thanks, most headaches

are healed, pleas for those in debt
or prison are sometimes granted,

requests for moratoriums on gravity
are denied; only ask and rain may fall,

but pancreatic cancer won't relent,
war prayers cancel each other out.

Men cry praying where I was born,
cry because the dying fetus is sad,

cry that Jesus suffered, dying for them,
cry especially hard at altar calls.

I see us in our early teens: guilt-ridden
by masturbation, stirred by scripture,

properly seasoned by hymns, sitting
as stoic as Buddhas through parables

of burning car crashes and morning
skid-row hangovers, of iron lungs

and abandoned women. And, if still
no one had come before him to kneel,

weeping copiously and confessing
egregious sins, Reverend Stallings

would signal the pianist to play more
gravely, softly, until the tune slowed,

minor arpeggios dropped their notes
like petals on an infant's coffin,

and in its well above the throat, the soul hurt.
The soul filled with tears, though how rarely

in such a small congregation would
anyone actually yield, repent, expose

the inmost privacy, when one might
march with hundreds down the sawdust

aisle at the annual countywide revival
and receive identical redemption

for the trifle of whispering to a stranger
and filling out a card. Then no more

fear of burning, no more worrying
sin's weird and pleasurable sensations.

And it lasts forever, this lasting peace
down deep, this grace of joining in,

infinitely renewable, sustaining grace
that hallows sluts and draws heroin

from addicts like toxin from a sting.
Its church is consecrated in the spirit,

and now there is even a bus to take
you there: Christian school, Christian

halfway house. The little sanctuary
has sprouted wings: staffed nursery,

kitchen and cafeteria, two ball
courts, web-mastered Christian internet,

bandstand for Christian heavy metal,
and widescreen Christian karaoke.

But no one shouts, it's not that kind of church.
The pews are walnut, the kneeling rails

are cushioned brass. They smile
as they sing. When they pray for you,

they mean it. They pray for keeps. They pray
to break your heart and make you one of them.

On Criticism

We praise it to entertain the idea that it should not have to exist.
That one song may yet last, that every man fails womanhood.
That each zebra masks an inadequate horse.

Pity ennobles the savage. For the ever considerate critic,
pity lacks aesthetic substance. Pity stands like a purple bridge
between the critic and the essence of the critique.

The ideal critic is stoical. Like a mailman,
he plods through the rain and never abandons his post.
A diction beagle, he secretly buries the word *numinous*.

No critic says "taste," though clearly that is the main thing.
The foundation of criticism is food.
Something missing from the sauce. We do not know what.

We taste its absence. Not the critic.
As the opera critic listens to the enlarged tenor
he works very hard to concentrate on the vocality of the banana split.

Without taste, criticism inflates to theory. The technique
and not the art. The theology without the religion.
The critic fails when he stops thinking of the sweetness.

After that, there is only the gift — the individual singing —
and the whole of creation, which proves nearly
impervious to criticism because of the peach.

Feelings, by Ashley Higgins

For every true emotion there is an objective
correlative. A rainy day, for instance,
might mean a person feels a little gloomy.
Or the convertible that carries the Peach Queen
from the parking lot of Kroger West
to the front lawn of the junior high school
could suggest a person's innermost feelings
about how the war goes on right in front of her
every night on CNN and all the other channels
and no one says what a dumb war it is,
the way no one comes right out and says
that the convertible girl became the Peach Queen
because she slept with one of the judges, Roy,
who maybe happens to be the ex-boyfriend
of the person writing the poem. I mean
many poems do not come right out and say
the feeling. They just give you the things.
A guy falls asleep in a bed of fire ants.
A girl with fake boobs rides in a convertible.
Another point is use things from real life.
As a child, when I felt moody, I would eat
half a caterpillar, and the other half
smushed up on my lower lip, the objective
correlative, I would show to the adults
who had made me sad, which reminds me
how later, if I hurt a child by accident
and the child began to cry and attack me,
I would throw myself against a tree or wall
and fall down and cry awhile myself

until the kid saw it and started to laugh,
though of course this did not work
for some people, like my cousin Dick,
who don't like poetry and never will —
they don't get it — the kind of people
who expect real smoke from a toy tractor.

The Elementary Principles of Rhetoric

The chief wonders of civilization were lies —
How else inveigle behemoths to work
and not split the gentle prophet's skull?
Newborns, maybe the first week, tell the truth.
After that it descends to propaganda.

Coos, grunts, *glurs,* germs of manifestos,
cries of the Valkyrie and warrior cults,
or laws streaming out of baby monitors
before words mount their charge
and end the dictatorship of the infant.

A little boy said: "I live in two worlds:
first is the world of authentic desires;
second, the world of universal dreams;
when big people take me out of the first,
I go to the world of universal dreams."

His father had asked me to speak with him.
He ignored arithmetic tests. On one
he had drawn a picture — when his teacher
asked what it was, he said, "A machine
that turns potatoes into billiard balls."

Problem. Problem — though not in my class —
little wizards, shamans, talented liars,
all wrote with pencils stolen many times.
On each pencil the teeth of every child
who ever held it had gnawed deep tracks.

The Heaven of Self-Pity

Clouds in the sky, rain on the streets —
They were talking about childhood.
Glum persons, orphans, blind from birth,
who after unconscionable abuses
in schools and numerous foster homes
were adopted by forensic psychologists.

Of my own childhood I recalled little.
A sickly boy, I hid and was not sought.
When I played dead, I was happiest.
I fell asleep and was devoured by mice.
Often I struggled with a jammed lock
in a car sinking through freezing water.

Clouds in the sky, rain on the streets —
The old couple who had taken me in
when my parents passed announced
at my grave that they had not known
until my kidnapping and torture
how special I was. The angels noted this.

Of course, they say that to everyone.
The struck, the caught, the blighted,
the cheated — it makes no difference
once you cross to the other side.
If you want mother, find some other heaven.
In the heaven of self-pity you are given a gun.

The Ante

A few sonnets about nature and the Greek gods.
Many free-verse poems in all lowercase letters.
Huey wrote of madness, Maddox of possums.
John played the sadness of empty stadiums.
Two berets, one silver-tipped cane, tweedy blazers.
In most Natalie poems, she took off her clothes.
The year of the Tet offensive. Wallace in Montgomery.
We read James Wright, Richard Wilbur, Anne Sexton.
One Friday an ex–guidance counselor from Jasper
leapt through the window of the cafeteria, shouting
"I am the son of Jesus Christ! Behold the Rapture!"
But nothing much happened in Poetry Writing 301
until Walter C. Avery wrote that a black swan,
born in the infralapsarian brain of a garbage dump,
would crack the codes of the Southern Baptists.
And for this jack-surreal, mildly apocalyptic truffle
was taken for near-genius material, practically
a second Edgar Allan Poe, until Sam Maisel
submitted his "Poem for the Worksheet Typist,"
which made everyone consider how scandalous
it must have seemed for her, a local woman,
a seamstress, and mother of Christian athletes,
to run across "I know you think you've seen it all before,
but this is duck rape, feathered love." And some,
in the critique afterward, praised the line endings;
one person even mentioned "The Second Coming,"
which, admittedly, made me blanch with envy,
so I wanted to say something about how
sometimes the subject is not what you think,

or the ones you imagine you are talking about
stand abruptly and begin to talk back to you,
but spring was bearing down on the workshop,
ripping out pages, grinding the opinions to nubs.
So much energy in the streets — demonstrations,
happenings, awakenings — so many instances
of sudden and involuntary enlightenment,
though mostly my friends and I spent our nights
on Sixth Street drinking beer at the Chukkar
or crouched in a huddle around a record player.
By the time I thought of Sam's duck again,
May had slipped into June and June into July,
and what is poetry in a copper tubing factory?
A cloud would fan out around the tubes
as the crane lifted them from the soaping vats
after they had softened in the furnace.
My job was to crimp a point on each of them.
Then the next man would carefully run them
through a die. Down the line I could see
the process repeating: the furnace, the point,
the die — the tubes and men diminishing.
All night the saws screeched and whined.
The pointers clattered. The press roared.
That was the beauty of it. You could sing.
No one would hear. You could say anything.

Confidential Advice

Jesus was full of it,
and Muhammad and the Buddha and Marx
(both Groucho and Karl)
and Mao Zedong and his fourth wife, Jiang Qing,
and Henry James said, "Three things
in human life are important.
The first is to be kind. The second is to be kind.
And the third is to be kind."
And in mid-practice, my elder cousin Dick Townsend took me aside,
propped himself on my shoulder pads,
and meticulously placing an elegant stream of chaw
between my winged shoes,
intoned in his slowly grunted Alabamian,
"Let me tell you something, honey.
If you know where you're going,
they do, too. Run reckless, son."
And Paul Bear Bryant, after having his construction-magnate buddies
from the Aggie Booster Club excavate a circular pit
forty feet deep and sixty feet across,
lowered two lean strips of human sirloin
down into the barbeque of the Texas August
and said, "First out starts. Now decide.
What's it gonna be boys, strength or speed?"
Well, it is hard, this advice, it is very hard.
And though few say, most agree
the woman who will make you better
(at love or work) is a lovely bitch
and the man to improve your presentation
and technique is a respected prick

who says what the world says: try
a little tenderness, and woe
to white and woe to black, and "Get back in there, turd.
You gotta shake off them heart attacks."

Starstruck

First came Bob (*Just-Bob*), a visiting cousin's
second husband, the operator
of Lyndon Johnson's teleprompter;
then Archie Persons, Truman Capote's
biological father,
jitterbugging in the parlor
at my eighth-grade English teacher's Christmas party.

Then more flagrant examples:
chance sightings of the spaceman
Wernher von Braun
and the *Hee Haw* star Junior Samples
before actual face-time
with Leonard Nimoy
and Joey Lauren Adams.

And why could I never speak directly?
Why that silly unworthiness
on confronting famous persons,
as if about to be auditioned
by the auditorium
of everyone who hated or loved them?

"And what was he really like?"
"Bald like Truman, but taller, older."
"Truman Potato," a boy

had said in class and the answer
rang as Archie danced — that glamour
as the thumbtacked hammers
rocked in Jean Skelton's upright piano.

The End of Practice

I had a dream of harnessing and exacting irrevocable power over others.
    It dissipated
or was usurped. But always I see it present-tense in the cleat-pocked, dried
    dirt of a practice field
where the coach is whistling us to prayer, the prayer rising like a black wing,
    the prayer,
and then the coachly speech, the whistle again, and then the last sprints.

The thirty-one young men line up together, there can be only one winner
    each time
they race to the light pole by the tennis courts and back, only one
    Achilles who will smile
and grimace back to the locker room that smells of the ammonia
    of unwashed practice jerseys
and stand for fifteen minutes under the pulsing jets of the shower and exult.

While the others posture or sag, then rise, lock in three-point stance,
    and, at the whistle, run,
each in his own fashion: the fat boys like buffalo, lurching blindly;
    the tall ungainly ones
with roseate elbows and aluminum shins; the Methodist minister's son;
    the stump with the ducktail
feigning lameness for the first seven races, then accelerating in the eighth.

For some it will never be the same: running, they have run out of words
    and now someone else
is telling the story: the footweight as though they struggled underwater
    shod in pond mud:

cottonmouth, lungfire, the white crud coagulating in the lip creases,
    the sticks of
Juicy Fruit and Doublemint grown flavorless, then granulating on the tongue.

Though one is still saying to the air with the radio announcer's voice
    of his childish
construction of valor, "He is dropping back; he is looking for an open
    man; they
have him; he is down. No, wait, ladies and gentlemen; no, he has broken
    a tackle; he is
running along the north sideline. Forty, thirty. There is only one man to beat."

How beautiful each becomes in loss. Jerry Reeder is vermilion. He is like
    a pale girl who has just made love.
Charles Sandlin is dark green. Richard Foot dapples. He is something
    by Manet or Seurat.
This is economics, pure and simple: the buying short, the selling high,
    and questions of timing:
Whose sweetheart is four months pregnant? Who is ill? Who broken?

I had the male dream. If I did not rise above the field, I would be eaten.
    At each moment
of my dream, I marked with shortening breath the dwindling likelihood
    of my flight —
"Battle," said Coach Pierce — that was the thing Blue Devils did: *battle,*
    and, while this came to pass,
monks in Asia soaked their robes in gasoline and burned alive for peace.

Winning

For my sister, excellence came naturally,
sewing dresses or speaking
brilliantly on safety or citizenship,
smiling and pushing buttons.
The only public competition
I ever won square and outright
was the 4-H Club sack race
at the old Morgan County fairgrounds.

Though this victory obtained
less from talent than the sack
I found wrapped around two
hundred pounds of cottonseed.
Catapult, warhorse, longbow, Gatling
gun, mustard gas, atomic bomb.
Emptied into humbler sacks,
it felt chastened, battle-ready.

My sister, when she won, beamed,
magnanimous in victory, graceful
at the podium as losers clapped.
As I ran past in the turbosack
the hoppers in the little bags
cast looks of shocked indignation,
and when I crossed the line,
I could not stop myself, I bowed.

This brought the ugly out. "Cheat!
Look at yourself in the mirror!"

one mother shouted while judges
huddled. New to winning,
this hurt my feelings, though
in the rush, they had made no rule
regarding size. If there is such
a rule, nowhere was it written.

Metaphors for the Trance

Because in play, of course, no one is going to die, not really,
at first it did not disturb me as we went at it on the rug,
both of us shaking our heads and snarling, he on top of me,

then I on top of him — a masque, a game like other games —
I would feint left, and he would feint right, baring teeth
as I parried with a French r from the back of my throat.

Except for the boundless whipping of his great wiry tail
and the mildly sebaceous odor of dog we might have seemed
two gentlemen before brandy and cigars fencing at the club.

Then I would play the beggar and he the rector in his carriage.
Then he the profligate younger brother and I the rightful earl,
rebuking him, "For Christ sake, man, do the civilized thing!"

But something in this act like night waves breaking on a jetty,
and all the time, his eyes brightening until I could sense,
in the brandishing of his shoulders and the brag of incisors,

some channel crossed, and, from farther in the dark, the part
that remained dark — not that millions would fall, it was not
the Battle of the Somme — he was a good dog and I his master.

We had played this game often — no bruising ever, never blood,
though it would prove tricky in the endgame to regain control:
I would have to draw him like a large key through a small hole.

Rememberer

You must understand,
long after the talking
ends, some voices
remain, and ghost
inside you in layers
like the voices you
remember bleeding
into one another under
the main conversation
on ancient telephones.

These voices, actual
people lived in them:
Geneva, Modena, Zora.
Einstein and Faulkner
agreed, once they met,
they heard such voices.
This word — any word,
without voices is lost.

And it works another way.
Le mot juste beneath
Mother's "My mind's
gone; my rememberer's
broke" is chicken fried
and chicken running.
In its beak, this chicken
holds a worm. "Worm,"

she said, leaning close
years ago — as it wriggled,
she said it again, more slowly.

Hubris at Zunzal

Nearly sunset, and time on the water
of 1984. Language its tracer.
No image like the image of language.

I had waded out about thigh deep.
Then a shout from the beach.
I held in my hand half a coconut shell

of coconut milk and 150-proof rum
and dumped it white into the waves
when it came on me how sweet it had been,

then the idea I was not finished,
then the act of reaching down
with the idea I would get it back.

Last Man Standing

The first cool nights, because we young loved
the young and loved living, at parties

you could see us trying on people like coats,
casting off those who did not fit or suit us,

then sidling to others we favored with fresh
strategies, our large dance moves in small

spaces, our philosophical chats in corners —
the rudiments of incompatibility cracking

like ice in a spring harbor until, at the hour
of pairing off, one by one, according to some

unspoken index of Darwinian excellence,
the couples would break away, the orders

of the beautiful and the suave, the wealthy
and the gifted, the tall and the sleek —

how utterly empty then the monastic
consolations of that shotgun apartment.

So Woolf and I would take off Van Morrison,
put on Coltrane and bring out the ouzo,

drinking without measure until one of us
might say "I," and after a few moments,

the other, "think," the syntax nodding
then in its nearly unconscious longing

for the sentence, and, in a while, maybe
"in any case," maybe "that," and the birds, the birds

IN MEDIA RES

Two Quick Scenes from the Late Sixties

1. COMPRESSION

Coming into Chicago, snow-scraps, street rigor
a mandatory visit before checking into the hotel
brick duplex apartment, Randy, PBR
(that yellow sweater, you Norwegian or what)
best time I ever had was in Vietnam Fortenberry
followed by odd moment, Triumph on sidewalk
Welcome to the Sheraton Blackstone, Sirs
Luggage? Wince, brown paper bag, wink
the governor's suite, three rooms, single-rate
stocked bar and complimentary poltergeists
of Damon Runyon and Amelia Earhart
Next day, a building, University of Chicago
dope smokers wainscoting both sides of the hall
at the end, a door, English Department
institutional decor of the grayest caliber
regulation woman, no one else, excuse me ma'am
we'd like to speak with Saul Bellow
unlikely, unlikely, segue, 10 A.M. tavern life
first time on the El, lunch in Plato's Cave
art museum, ice cream, bookstore near the Biograph
Merwin, *Postwar Polish Poetry,* Miller Williams
Brooks Brothers Sir, I can only offer
you might want to look in our boys' department
shame and Old Town daiquiris, pardonnez-moi
he always orders in French, license check
whores real actual whores in the alleys
What's your name, Fancy, that's cold

I mean, what's your last name, Strawberries
before a stop at a liquor store, Frost 8/80
clear white liquor, heaven on earth elixir
drink all night, wake, and no hangover
the next day, crossing into Indiana, Gary
a hallucination, Indianapolis labyrinthine
block on block, devoid of landmarks or signage
and U.S. 31, the beeline, buzzing to a stop
in a parking lot behind a boarded-up pawnshop
where we piled out stinking to witness above us
the purple cross of the annual Easter air show
and agreed indeed that might well be a sign
it might be time to have that talk with Jesus.

2. THE RUSH

began much earlier, a party at Time's house, people going in
and coming out, relationships changing, clever words

being spoken in every room and then at an unanticipated
moment of implosive malaise Time asked, Do you smoke a pipe

Interesting assortment there: meerschaum, clay, Italian briar
metallic curios fashioned clandestinely in penitentiary

machine shops, tubing and thimble contraptions studded
with clock gears, costume jewelry, head shop bric-a-brac

Please don't go to any trouble, whereon Time produced
a cabinet, the kind mechanics keep to file screws and bolts

of sundry dimensions, a number of sliding drawers
arranged vertically, in each drawer ranks and files of little

silver tins, in each tin a powder or a finely manicured
dried vegetable matter, an anthology of spices

an apothecary from which Time drew, as meticulously
as a geisha at a tea ceremony, fine leaves and pinches

and filled the bowl, the room full of us waiting then
smoking until it seemed all there was in the world

was this wonderful naked guy playing the harp and his naked
wife crooning in the key of D minor *Tyger, tyger in the night*

Quite an accomplishment, a great blessing, thank you, absolutely
splendid before the soprano cracked and fell to bass

a tambourine went bird, beards changed faces
a flower from the carpet rose and clung to the wall

a sprinkle perhaps of phencyclidine extruding the hours
an eye inside a foot, the foot changing to a mountain,

two beautiful boys at a mirror, exchanging masks
a girl crying, repeatedly, it is never going to end

and someone said Time was to blame and someone else
said Time had disappeared and another, look at the light

though the thing is, of course, as they say, it was not the visuals
so much as the subtle changes that accrued in the philosophy

or as Alice noted, returning from the restroom, it seems as if
a hundred years have passed, and Electro said, but it is still

now it is always now, and with his hoop blew out a bubble
and now, said Time, now for a shotgun of the really dynamite stuff

The Essence of Man

What kind of person would hate the color blue,
hate the salesman who jiggles change and the nurse
who murmurs with the voice of a little girl
and the leg that cannot sit a minute without making
a minor tremor register on the Richter scale;
hate infants in general and conversation starters;

hate thongs, medallions, ice cubes, conservatives,
mayonnaise, mouth breathers, foreplay,
pencil tappers, and burkas; hate both *The Iliad*
and *The Odyssey*, and delivery vans, and the idea
of dowries; hate plum sauces, exclamation
marks, train crossings, and funeral flowers?

And how could a person hate cuckoo clocks
and text messaging; hate wedding parties
and David Letterman; hate the day of the week;
hate both the beauty pageant and the ugly stick;
hate equitably the chihuahua and the Jell-O salad;
hate jazz patch, Vandyke, and Fu Manchu?

In an age of mercury and mass extinctions,
what sort of citizen would expend her hate
on the double pleat and the star-nosed mole,
on parade floats and essays on public radio;
would abhor people named Tiffany or Dale,
and beckon the handsome, articulate waiter, *O Enjoy*?

How could a person act that way? The candidate
for national office is introducing the family
of the dead fireman who rescued a schoolhouse.
The famous baseball player is pointing to heaven
as he rounds first base. The Beatles harmonize.
The inspirational speakers are shopping for boats.

Surely it would be counterproductive to hate
nicknames, elevators, and remote controls;
to speak out against body piercings and snowmobiles;
utterly ridiculous to detest weekends
because, on Sunday, it is necessary to rise early
to beat the whistler to the grocery store.

O it must be terrible not to have a Mexican,
not to have a great Satan or a lunatic Muslim,
some gay person or Jew, but to have to make do
with the rain and one squeaking wiper blade,
O gods of carnage and inestimable slaughter,
the smell of Brut, the taste of coconut.

Deathly

I am alone, driving through St. Louis,
listening to a ballad by Aimee Mann.
There is a fine romance to listening to loud rock 'n' roll
as you drive a late-model car through a big city late at night:
the ordinary nostalgia, with its useless longing,
and then the clearer nostalgia for what never happened:
Februaries in Rio, blind tropical sweethearts,
the last few treaties of the Gore administration.
It is acceptable for once to be a fool.
It is totally awesome to have come
from Rolla and to be going to Carbondale.
A cool rain has fallen for most of the day
and now the road glitters with that light
that indicates spring and Eros and things going by:
the Hill, Busch Stadium, then Saarinen's arch;
certain parties in 1973, embraces by banisters, day trips;
many times shining. "It is too late," the music says
without coming right out and saying it. "It is hopeless
and it will never again be so beautiful." A girl
once played this very song for me and told me
it made her think of me, a thing that nearly broke my heart,
though, in fact, it was herself she meant.
The singer alone is the subject of the song.
The rest is only love, for which I remain an idiot.
I think of Neruda's mongoose nearly every day.
Of old girlfriends weeping at my funeral.
Of what Keats wrote to Fanny Brawne,
and how much it pleased me, on May 17, to write in a journal:
"Setting words on top of music

is like placing a fat man on a small pony."
But now as I drive, and I am not supposed to be anywhere,
the words raise that girl, and then myself,
exalted, her attention gilding my ego like rain,
until I begin thinking of other women
together in a car late at night, and of my grandmother,
and her friends, humming as they quilted
scraps of guano sacks and overalls,
how they had already drifted away from me
when I came out of the Holland Tunnel in 1971.
So as I cross the Mississippi, I play it again,
three times, and then again, a lucky man,
alive in the dark country, singing along,
driving with my lights out for the fun of it.

In Media Res

Of the one instant we might die in, if we consider it,
it has not yet happened or it is too late, and what
seems to remain of it after an hour misses the point,
and twenty years after it is like twenty years before:
a mud dauber buzzing, the burn smell off the miter saw,
some warp in the quotidian where our talk
migrated to the Steelers, midmorning light
striped and angled by the odd bunching of the shades.

That the husband was sick, gravely ill, we did not know yet
or much of that place beyond the hardwood floor,
tongue-and-groove red oak in nearly flawless condition,
which I had bought for a dollar a foot
and that we were prying up from the underlayment
of the house the couple had moved out of into a trailer
where they were living while the carpenters
framed in the new house across the road.

From all we could see, he was just thin, nothing extraordinary
in his talk, a young farmer with an education.
She was the one who got our attention,
large and blond, easy with others and herself.
If you read *Beowulf* and come to the place
where Wealhtheow, Hrothgar's queen, moves among the men,
pouring mead in the great hall, there is the grace I mean.
And where could we go with that?

Only that a respect accrued from watching her
tow a wagon across the lawn, pivot, and back it into the barn.

A pleasure to see her hoeing or petting the dog.
And when she spoke, a lightness to her voice, no hint —
though later we would agree we should have known,
so gray was his face, so drawn his mouth
when he dropped by, saying how his mother had kept the house,
the kitchen spotless, the floor always shiny and lemon-scented.

Or perhaps we denied it or knew subliminally,
wedging a crowbar under each board, leaning back
and rocking gently to save the wood from splintering —
the Midwest cocked outside, the wind carving runnels in the wheat,
and farther, the identical fields repeating, the houses
clean and functional, each with its outbuildings,
farm implements, and farrowing pens — and then
one day he said, "This hospital shit is bad for business."

The good humor of a dying man is worth something.
I do not say what. We took the floor. Courage?
Beauty? *Leukemia*, she said, *bone marrow*,
but not like sorrow, more like the dust
shaken from the boards by the violence of the saw,
the particles before us, distinct, then nothing.
More tests, she said, and *hope* — the evidence
was there in the rooms going up across the field.

What Is True for a Minute

My alien in Alabama was an invisible noise,
a *whoof* or a *heeraah* that rose from the ground
or hovered in the air, and I attempted to talk
with it, first in English, then with songs,
"Love Me Tender" and "Town Without Pity,"
then with the sounds that are not words.
When I went left, it moved to my right.
When I went right, it was behind me again.
It was like the alien in North Carolina
that coughed from the upstairs apartment
where no one lived, except the alien
in North Carolina was a clanking radiator
while the Alabama alien was the noise
of the drain from the washing machine.
In El Salvador an alien followed me one night
when I was angry and drunk and intending
to walk the beach to Baja California. It
swung a machete over its head, a *shurr* and a *hish*,
and when I stopped to plead for my life,
it turned into a crab, scuttled across the sand,
and vanished under a pile of driftwood.
None of my aliens stay long. Mostly,
I was lonely when I saw them. I was sad
or scared or the breath had been knocked from me.
Once a wall spoke. A deer instructed me.
A retriever looked at me with the eyes
of my newly dead friend, and staring back at it,
I thought of how the gods appeared to men
except my aliens were never gods. One

was a shadow. One was a cottonmouth underwater.
My alien in Sorrento was a real woman,
almost a girl from early Yeats, but in jogging shorts,
she moved down the steps to the sea —
she was from the earth, but also of the air,
and, as she began running lightly, a light rain
from down the coast Amalfi began taking
the parts of her and stirring them into mist.
I think she was a figure for desire or fear
who came into the world for a minute
and disappeared forever. That is the way
with aliens, all evanescence, all difference —
unknowable presences, enemies of description,
they wait and their work is seeming.
They speak with the voice of listening.

The Previous Tenants

1

The couple who built our house had great plans
for this lot where they would live out their days:
he in dedicated husbandry, priming a garden
with sludge from the sewage plant, hauling stones
from the condemned homesteads by the new lake
to buttress the terraces; and she reading Aquinas
or pouring Pinot Noir for predinner conversations
after her work as a counselor at the women's center.
She had returned to school late, a fourth degree,
and a meaningful career after years of jobs
for little pay or credit, the fate of a faculty wife.
She had a gift for empathy, a true calling,
said a fellow counselor at her memorial.
And then the younger son stood and agreed that, yes,
she was a fine counselor, but a terrible mother.
"She was not there for us when we failed.
She only loved our successes." Cicadas,
then October's first cold night, the instant
stuck there like an arrow singing in a wall.

2

Until then we had foolishly thought them happy:
he an accomplished man, a graduate of Penn;
and she a woman of privilege and beauty,
tall and regal with aquiline nose and blue eyes.
On the few occasions I saw them together,

she made him, by comparison, seem dull.
Later, after he died, I would see her sometimes
at retirement dinners, and we would talk.
She liked to tell of meeting Franklin Roosevelt —
just that once, but she remembered,
she said, how he threw his head back like a horse,
and laughed — "a high horse-laugh,"
she described it each time, though the joke,
which I only dimly recall, was on her.
She seemed pleased that we got the house.

3

It would suit us fine if there were a bathroom
guests could use without first going through a bedroom.
The big room upstairs, open and high-ceilinged,
a luxury after the cedar frame and plain brown door,
as though the modest exterior held a larger interior.
The screen porch, the south-facing windows
that let in light's various shades of romantic contentment;
neighborly amenities, houses set back from the street,
three-acre lots, trees and flowers, and always the deer
materializing out of the maples and walnuts
that curtain us from each other and grant solitude
until November when the leaves fall.
The walkers happening by, sometimes a barred owl,
or an eagle, or one of the hawks that nest in the woods by the lake.
George, a friend of theirs, asked for clippings of columbine

planted along the drive, and when
we could not find them, he insisted,
so we looked again, but found nothing.
What we know is a garden and a calendar:
daffodils at winter's end, then forsythia, azaleas,
purple irises half a week before yellow, and each year,
on the seventh of May, peonies, of a lustrous salmon,
like cones of sherbet at the back of the lawn.

4

He forgot the names of the irises, but the ego did not diminish.
He forgot the trowel under the azalea, but the ego did not diminish.
He forgot the azalea. Others and then himself he forgot.
The byzantine roads to town and the apple tree he forgot,
the dogwood and the cherry, and his key to Jerusalem,
but the ego did not diminish. Often it seemed to him
he was here, he looked into the goldfish pond and saw
himself, but it was the wrong year, the pond was gone.
It was cold and hot at once, the hours ran together,
and he wanted Mother, but the ego did not diminish.
He thought toward names almost here, tools and angels.
He pruned the forsythia's wilderness of rain shoots.
He rode into town for grass shears, but at the corner
of Sycamore and Oakland, turned right instead of left,
and then, after a block, left, and began to drive in a dream
of a bay, past the topiary hedges and manicured lawns
in the neighborhood of his childhood and knew

it was not a dream and parked in the shade and waited
until the officer came, but the ego did not diminish.
He forgot his Blake, his "Little lamb, who made thee?"
And "I see all things, past, present and future."
He forgot the gold of his wife's skin illumined.
The ego did not diminish, but the skull rose,
and the garden came to her, a displaced city girl.
She saw beauty in work and gratitude in mourning.
She rubbed her hands together and looked at the sky.
The dragon horticulture squatted on her back.

5

How do you know you are old?
Lung ache. Arrhythmia. Temporary
aphasias. The tap left dripping —
second, hour, day, week, month,
Vicodin, Vytorin, Crestor —
rhythms of looking and forgetting:
the instant in spring
when the sun overcomes
the effects of the wind
and the instant in fall
when the wind overcomes
the effects of the sun — one year
would be a good way to see it
if you could see a year.
"The first year of marriage,"

Borden Plunkett's uncle told him,
"each time you make love,
place a penny in a jar.
The second year,
begin taking them out.
When the jar is empty,
you will be old."

6

Most of us who live here do not come from here
and seem to be somewhere else when we talk
and would not know a hackberry from a cottonwood
though we post e-lerts for copperhead sightings
and eschew Dursban and Diazinon, which explains
the surfeit of moles and brown recluse spiders.
"How do you like it there?" friends often ask,
and it always surprises, I think of it so little,
only occasionally when I walk, that some places
are better, others worse: vague thoughts
with a negotiable distance between them, the way towns
cropped up east of the Mississippi every six miles,
the time it took by horse and wagon to come and trade
and get back with light to milk and feed the stock.
So many histories, hoofed and creeping beneath the wheel.
The Shawnee, then the French, then the English.
Peach orchards west of us, mariachi from the trailers,
and under us the black übershelf of anthracite,

fallow since the late-seventies EPA restrictions.
Miners out of work, meth freaks, holy rollers.
And our suburb like a little blue island in a red sea:
philosophers and psychologists, a mathematician from Cameroon,
an Algerian theorist, three attorneys, a Belsen survivor
with her wristlet of numbers — realtor, sculptor,
photographer, car salesman, anesthesiologist.
Fundamentalists, freethinkers, Muslims, Jews.
The dreamed peace a little money makes possible. Bells
of the ice cream truck. Wild turkeys in the yard.
Fiction, said Forster, is what others think we are.

7

We know them from the colors they left more than their words.
We know them more from the marks they left on the wood
than the pulses that quickened when they entered rooms.
We know the four flower beds. We do not know their love.
We know all that went unrepaired and fell apart.
We know them from others more than they told us themselves.
From all that he left unfinished, we know how he began not to know.
We know from the ripped-out risers of the stairwell,
from the basement clothesline and boxes of bolts and screws.
From instruction manuals and extension cords, we know.
From sprung traps and expired poisons, from loose wire.
How small the distance to our neighbors across history.
We tell their time by the birdfeeder rotting on its post.
From the oak log in the gully, we know their shade.

From things that work and things that no longer work.
From lapsed warranties, from fire alarms in every room.
From the nail the Sheetrock still grips, the stove's vortical eyes.
From plastic that each winter sealed in the screen porch.
From a light wheelbarrow, a bulb planter, a rusty awl.
From the foundation crack, we know their charity for the cedar.
What we do not know and what they know will be one thing.
It hooks and trims us. It weighs us in the blackbird's flight.

8

Going back a year, and another year,
I am recovering from rotator-cuff surgery.
I have a ball, with which I am instructed
to roll letters onto a door. I have decided
during this time, because I neglected it
as a child, to learn the alphabet backward.
Some of the sequence is hard to remember.
I keep stopping at S and J. The blocks
are not plaque, I think. These oubliettes
in the backward alphabet stopped me in 1955.
Some of the letters hurt. X is electric,
a hard, tingling jolt. W is unforgivable.
The son's story bothers me because it is not nice.
I was raised not to say things that give offense,
a cultivated mind, a garden of beautiful words
like *A Child's Garden of Verses* on the shelf;
and, under the euphemisms, a paralysis

of cordialities, so for my sister and me
it was never possible to have it out.
As if the soul were better left private,
our mother pointed to the intractable God,
to be worshiped publicly, prayed to in silence.
The usual Protestant thought. With others
we were always wrong. Only in solitude could we be right.

9

Some things to pray to in the Shawnee Hills:
homesteads under Cedar Lake, the breath in soldiers' graves,
the preemptory faith of the ill and alcoholics.
I think of another story from the wife's memorial service.
She was angry with her husband when he died.
Piques. Rages. Petulances. All that wrongheadedness
the doctors had forbidden her to correct when he was alive.
A friend suggested that she write him a letter.
The letter of inanimate jealousy, the caregiver's self-love.
In all, it took a little more than a month,
and then they spaded a hole and buried it under a rose.
We had meant to strip the place of their presence.
Downstairs we ripped out the acoustic tiles and put up car siding.
Hardwood floors over the cement. We halved the large
room where guests slept: a bedroom for Alexis, and for me
a study with built-in bookshelves. A calm place to write.
Morning accompaniment of cardinals. But late at night
I think of exhuming that letter. Yesterday

when I stepped out to smoke, four deer were lying on the lawn
and I thought her words or his spirit had entered the deer.

10

When people die, you look for them beside you
and find them sometimes in the hawk's eyes,
and then back, back into the cloud, the shape of vanishing.
Something today in the in-box that does not apply,
that slipped the title-grabbers of the spam filters —
She didn't know anything about the Einstein theory.
She loved to pore over the advertisement pictures in the magazines.
The bite and tang of the cold air seemed to increase her anger.
There were long pauses when she lay very still —
and yet applies nearly and completely by accident
so spirit in one of its digital avatars seems involved,
and voices rush in, other people's and my own.
All day I hear them as I go about my chores.
We believe when a person dies, said Golda Meir, a world dies.
Silent genesis, fawn of the afterlife, articulate mist,
what do the ghosts say to dreams? Vagrant loneliness
of the inner stairway, transmission of liniment and salve,
language of original starlight that we unknowingly quote —
the thought nearest the doing works best. Measure,
then measure again, and the third nails it. I lay
new walkway over old path, place new boards in old fence.
When a new thought goes against an old one, deny neither.
The wood with its resins still speaks of the tree.

I find black slats in the screen porch where she sat
and little oblong holes of transparency like runs in stockings.
I fix things because they are here and in the distance.
With a utility knife, I score the wire and break it off,
cut new slats to length, paint them, and climb the ladder.

Cathedral

Over time it occurs to me
I am building a shed that will burn.
Footer and sill, whatever I do
flames blue and translates to ash.
The nail shrieks as it enters the joist
and streams out, shrieks
and drips a metal tear
from the elemental eye.

What I do not know is here.
I worship wood and the instant.
What is over, I can never finish.
The angel of work is sweat.
And still as I move the brush
many faces look back at me.
The stain vanishing into the knot
reminds me of something I forgot.

RELIQUARY OF THE OTHER WORLD

The Art of Heaven

In the middle of my life I came to a dark wood,
the smell of barbecue, kids running in the yards.
Not deep depression. The nice hell of suburbs.
Speed bumps. The way things aren't quite paradise.
Nights I read Speer's *Inside the Third Reich*. He made
Hitler so amiable. It seemed important to see that.
There had been a murder in town. The victim
was Lucia's student, a naturalist and promising poet.
Jealousy on steroids. Spying. Stalking. Threats.
Then violence of such a brutal, dehumanizing kind,
I felt the need to submerge the killer in a pattern.
A friend said the connection between depression
and humor was genetic. Because the mother
was often sad, the child learned to tell her jokes.
I wondered if the killer played an instrument.

Coming home each afternoon past the dairy farm,
and the three curves before Union Hill Church,
I kept rewinding and viewing evidence from his trial:
the break-in, the stabbing, the new friend helpless,
listening as she asked, "Am I going to die now?"
and then hearing, "Yes, you're going to die now."
Multiple slashes, cuts, nicks on the bone of the spine.
I saw the little pains coming up from the big pain like smoke.
The horses grazing in the field did not raise their heads.
Earlier she had been eating pizza in a place near campus.
He drank a few beers in a bar where I go sometimes.
Perhaps I had once bumped into him as I threaded
through the pool tables on the way to the men's room.

Or was that her, alone in a corner, studying his letter
that began, "Tramp, liar, whore, enchantress, bitch."

Now you can find it on the internet — it reads like
a farce of the ego or a sample of Leviticus — "Eternal
lover . . . [I will] come crashing down —" in the records
of the circuit court of Jackson County, Illinois — "with
a thunderous vengeance and a furious anger —" sad
brackets where the characters grew indecipherable
as the author's hand hastened or trembled — "and they
will know that my name is Houdini because I can
disappear and reappear like magic and no man —"
Here a mother might still help. Here I see a boy
with air guitar, lip-synching, strutting at a mirror —
"nor beast nor nothing manmade can either contain or hold me."
But where the posturing ends, the blade is whetted,
and the inner geniuses begin to work for an idiot,
all the editors wade into the still waters of sleep.

The bar was quiet in the afternoons, and later,
the noise of the racks breaking. On the televisions
above the tables, the images of men running
back and forth and crashing into each other —
I thought that for him her death had started as a game,
that the game took the form of possession, a trance,
as on childhood nights when the room and hour vanish.
That the process is the same for the many as for the one,
the beauty, the beguilement, then the blindness.
That this projection might be reversed or spun.

You could look at blood and see the art of heaven.
Probably you could see it. You could not confess.
Even in the bunker, Hitler saw himself as architect.
Speer, in the Cathedral of Ice, directed the lights
skyward to hide the homeliness of the Gauleiters.

The Moons: Notes on the Formation of Self

An old couple in Wednesday-night Bible study —
the Moons, David and Ella, they would be dead now,
I can write about them. We were discussing the Apostle Paul,
a single man, with many ideas about marriage
and one or two about divorce, and the Moons,
recent converts — they had both been married before —
began to cry, as many cried in those services
because they believed they were going to hell.
Ralph Alexander was our pastor. For us, his flock,
his congregation, in addition to preaching,
he built cabinets and tuned-up cars. Because of him,
I try not to get too excited about the idea of being dead.
In the air, particularly, when the turbulence happens
on a vacuum and the plane drops precipitously,
as long as the jolt softens and the carry-ons
stay in their bins and the stewards are not crying.
It helps, also, to think of Wallace Stevens writing near
the end of his life, "It is an illusion that we were ever alive."
The Moons fly with me, too, on the wing crying,
and maybe I put them here because the Moons,
in their intensity, remind me of suicide bombers.
What do you think? Do you have a self, a soul, an option
all your own and not just what others received
and passed on, installing it in you as one ape
will cry and another ape take it and make the same noise —
And is it fair to include the Moons' cries among the ape cries?
Are you one of the ones gravely offended
to hear the human creature, made in the image of God,
represented as an ape? Would you prefer coyote?

Last year coyotes ate one of our neighbor's dogs,
a little gray and white terrier, Bandit — one night
chained to the doghouse with his name on it,
and the next, just the chain and the gnawed-on spine.
I hear them at night, a chorus of otherworldly *fatwas*,
fugues, and arias, and sometimes one of them
will shift and take the voice of another
the way the Moons shifted when they read Paul's letter.
No one has told me this, I have thought of it on my own.
The rain is falling and the gutters do not hold all the water —
Friends, anything all your own? — a scrap, even
a whole indiscretion you whisper sidelong to your buddies —
Do you secretly want them to pass it on to others?
Do you want them to use your name in connection with it?
Do you sometimes lower your voice to be overheard?
I pass the Moons on to you, the virgins in paradise,
and three of the men who flew the planes into the towers
who visited strip clubs the week before their martyrdom.
When the people I think of as myselves talk to me
of the suicide bombers, the one with the muscle car
and the tattoo of General Nathan Bedford Forrest
suggests to the one pretending to be Mahatma Gandhi
that when a person carries a bomb strapped to his chest
into a market and sets it off, or releases sarin
in a subway tunnel, it might be a good idea,
since the person cannot be stripped naked
and dangled upside down in a freezing room,
and since there will never be a chance to take a file
and grind away the teeth or to tie the body down

and douse it in honey and set it near a bed of fire ants
or to open little wounds and pour in mercury or Liquid-Plumr,
that it might be a good idea to kill first the bomber's
mother and father, then all the children, the mates,
all the uncles and the aunts, the cousins to the seventh remove,
that this would be humane, less murderous than war.
Because of what I heard that Ralph Alexander told the Moons,
I resolve that there are many selves, some bad,
some good, that it is important to hear them all
and say their names in secret and let them go.
I did not see the Moons enter the parsonage before dawn.
I do not know what to believe, but I believe
that Ralph Alexander told the Moons to disregard
that one instance of holy scripture, no matter —
They would not have to separate in order to go to heaven.

The Poem of Fountains

1

Bill Turley asked me to sit on the board of the Lilac Basin Sewage
    Corporation —
    I was working on a poem about fountains,
but Bush had just claimed Florida; it felt timely to say yes and wax
    respectable.

2

The annual meeting brought neighbors who typically kept to themselves:
    world citizens, impresarios;
the union man, Morteza Daneshdoost; the rocket scientist,
    Tsuchin Philip Chu.

3

The system, said Chu, works by gravity: at the nadir, an electric pump;
    three eight-by-fourteen
reinforced-concrete holding tanks; a control panel of switches and
    capacitors.

4

A brisk day, everyone chatting, we pulled on boots and walked the line.
    In the flow field beyond the lagoon,
I noted three varieties of fountains: willow, buttercup, wild iris.

5

Over coffee and beignets, the board traced its origins to a Marxist
    historian, a descendant of John Adams.
Come officer-selecting time, I accepted the vice presidency.

6

In the event of an obstruction I would greet the city truck
    and chat with the crew while they slipped
a hose into a cleanout and blasted a channel through the roots.

7

A few weeks into my tenure, our president, Jean Boehne, on the phone—
    The obstetrician had ordered bed rest
for her pregnant daughter-in-law. Soon she would fly to Colorado.

8

Three days into Boehne's absence, a red light flashing. Tanks
    erupting. Sewage backing up
in basements, the suddenly outed air of the underground.

9

In times of extraordinary stress, wrote the *New York Times*
    of W and his administration,
the ordinary man may summon unprecedented greatness.

10

But moments of high valor remind me of fountains, the ego cresting
    as the surge of dailiness falls back.
When I see myself at that time, I am like a fountain as I rush to the phone.

11

And as I start to dial, *plumber?, electrician?*, the two numbers run together
    and I remember Turley's caveat:
"It can prove interesting, in this neck of the woods, which Williams to call."

12

Events to regard dispassionately: the concrete lid of the last holding tank
    would not sustain a man on a Bobcat;
the truck full of bilge was too heavy for the bridge by the Hickman-Porter's.

13

A friend said "shit patrol" to describe the board of the sewage corporation,
    probably not meaning anything pejorative —
"Turd blossom, high prophet, Quasimodo," Bush addressed his cabinet.

14

Though mostly when I think of Bush, I see Li'l Abner's idol, Fearless Fosdick,
    blowing away innocent bystanders
and capturing the mayor while the actual thugs smirk down the back stairs.

15

If the young jazz guitarist Bill Frisell was making too much of a burlesque
    of comping beside him,
the maestro, Jim Hall, would say, "Don't just play something; stand there."

16

Some are no good with decisions. Boehne is good with decisions. I am
    effective
    with the snake when the line
to the flow field stops up; also, I do not hesitate to put my hands in the stuff.

17

When Jung observed that the human being remains three years old all its life
    perhaps he meant
that the imagination never stops constructing the behavior of the mythical
    adult.

18

How far shy of this great one we fall. But how like a fountain our vote
    to restore the control panel. How uplifting
the thrust of the second pump. How elegant the waste pooled in the lagoon.

The Trip to Opelika

My always smiling sister, who once stopped a corporation
from digging a granite quarry across the road from her house,

my father, who loves good stories and jokes
and took to reading John Grisham after he went deaf,

and my mother, who isn't clear on the last thing
she said but remembers everything seventy years ago,

are riding along in my car south of Birmingham
and my mother is talking about Grandma Kitty,

how tough it was for her in the years before the Depression
with her husband dead and five kids to raise,

what a good mother she was and how she
persevered in the midst of unthinkable adversity,

moving the whole family by horse and wagon
from Georgia and making a life, though I wonder

at times how good a mother she could have been,
seeing how, on a childhood rabbit-hunting trip,

Uncle Manson shot Uncle Cecil in the back
so he was paralyzed from the waist down

and had to hop around on crutches for the rest of his life
and another brother whose name no one can remember now

rolled off the porch in his wheelchair, suffering
a brain injury from which he never recovered,

but I do not say anything, as once on another ride
when I raised this very point, Mother puffed up

and took a ninety-seven-mile vow of silence —
as I do not suggest to my father that, if he likes John Grisham,

he should try reading Dostoyevsky or at least John McPhee,
or better still, a poetry collection, and my father does not

lecture me on how I should attend church once in a while
or at least pretend to care more about the Lord,

so we let Mother carry on about Grandma Kitty.
"Think of her, a lone woman," she says as we are riding

along past Alabaster and decide to stop for a meal
in one of those places where there is so much grease

in the chicken-fried steak you get the feeling
there is a line from the filling station to the kitchen,

and my father has the small sirloin, adding copious
amounts of salt even though after he fell seven feet

from a loading dock more than twenty years ago,
he has no sense of taste or smell but always adds

the salt because he says he cannot imagine the taste
without it and everyone compliments the waitress

and then we drive on south, my mother going on all the time,
Grandma Kitty did this Grandma Kitty did that,

and me thinking we should be talking about Uncle Luke,
who late in his life as a hobby took to riding around

and when he saw a kid skipping school would offer
the kid a ride and take him to Decatur and turn him in to the truant officer,

or Grandpa Nesmith, the atheist, who hand-planed his own
cedar coffin and sat beside it on the front porch his last years,

complaining to anyone who passed about Social Security
and hypocrites and church ladies and terrible preachers —

except that these are the manly stories my father would tell
and being deaf he does not say much now though

his mind is sharp as ever so we get Mother to holler
to him when we do not know which road to take

or we cannot settle an argument about the name
of a third cousin's second wife's adopted nephew,

and occasionally my sister will maybe pipe in —
she runs an antiques shop now — about some

eight-thousand-dollar post-Edwardian table covered with
nine layers of green paint that she found in front

of a fabric store and argued the man down to six dollars
after he first asked twelve, and our father will smile

as though he could hear, or because it is a clear night
in a long, good life, he can see the signs for Opelika,

and Mother says she remembers that table,
a remarkable table, Grandma Kitty had one a lot like that.

The Eviction

My privilege to have witnessed this, so late in the middle
  of the twentieth century
that already it seemed historical, almost like having seen
  Erasmus or Thucydides:
a shack at the end of a field road, an eczema of garden,
  domineckers on the porch —
the whole place stank of sweat, coal oil, and excrement,
  and under it, the ghosts
of things rotted and desiccated so far past the organic
  there remained only
the stark elemental testimony of sulfur and ammonia.

Why were we there? Because the wife, the principal filth,
  big-man big
and raccoon mean, had been bootlegging and pimping
  the grown daughters,
and the husband, the little cross-eyed gimp with the chaw
  mark like a burn scar
down the neck creases, who might have been the father
  of seven or eight
of the fourteen living children, liked to lay up drunk
  while the udders
of the Jerseys wilted and Johnson grass choked the cotton.

What else? Feuds, wrecks, debts, petty thieveries, arm-
  twistings, and beatings —
When my grandfather, at the behest of my grandmother,
  told the woman to get out,

she had sulled up, there had been a quarrel, a death threat;
    he had taken out a warrant,
and now that the thirty days of the warrant had expired,
    and he might
physically evict them, move their belongings out of the house
    and set them on the road,
with what care they loaded these things onto the wagon.

First the brown sofa with the springs working out of it,
    then the cable-spool table,
cane chairs nailed together or bound with baling twine,
    fruit jars, kettles, and pots —
A straining and grunting with eyes — but the girl Sheila —
    she was my friend —
and Paul — he would go to college and become something —
    an architect? an engineer?
With what omissions do I lard memory? By what secret
    jurisprudence
do my inner committees invent logic and a sentence?

Almost half a century, what does it matter that the terrible
    mother of sharecroppers
who prayed to Bacchus to become anything other than rows
    of cotton
has turned into a stand of pines and risen into a paper factory?
    The shack is gone.
One night three drunk volunteer firemen came and set a fire
    to practice putting it out.

I know the man who puts his neighbor out in the road

    is a cold son of a bitch,

yet I am no sweeter than my grandfather. I study the ground.

North Alabama Endtime

Earlie has come to my house
on Sunday in a Chevy Nova
to say that the world is ending.
"Anyone can see it," he says.
"The signs are right before us,
your global warming,
your famine and pestilence,
your jihads and holy wars."

"I don't know," I say to Earlie.
"Maybe the physics guys see it —
quarks, muons, neutrinos —
the building blocks of matter
are naked as pole dancers
to those geniuses, but us,
we read but we're ignorant.
We're like goats eating paper."

"No, it's scripture," says Earlie.
"It's right there in Revelations.
The world is going to end.
You've hardened your heart."
"People are going to cry," says
Earlie's oldest boy, Tabor,
and looks straight at me,
"for the rocks to fall on them."

"I can nearly see that," I tell Tabor.
"People get depressed. It seems

like there's no way out, but then
maybe they let it go a day,
something fantastic happens,
they change prescriptions,
a redhead moves to town —
yesterday I saved a turtle's life."

"You're too negative about
the end of time," says Earlie.
"It's like anything different.
You have to give it a chance,
strike while the iron is hot.
And it's hot, it's very hot.
The battle of Armageddon
has probably already started."

"I'd like to be more positive,"
I say. "And I try. I really do.
I read all I can about wars
and the evil in men's hearts,
but it's tough with the end.
It's like the championship,
Nothing is playing Infinity.
It looks to me like a dead tie."

"You're wrong," says Tabor.
"Good triumphs in the end."
"He's got you there," says Earlie.
"Good always whips evil's ass.

Just wait. People are going
to weep and gnash their teeth.
Not that you will," he says.
"You're thinking. That's a start."

"I hope it's not too late," I say
and wave as they drive off,
not bad men, disturbed maybe,
but like all Turrentines, friendly.
You can say anything to them.
Probably they just got carried away.
They meant to talk politics.
The end of time was just a pretext.

Lines for the Joe Wheeler Rural Electric Cooperative

They say the other world is in this one, but they don't say what.
It looks like there is a screen over it.
Everything moving, if only we could see it more closely.
Time the barrier and allower.
It looks like we're in it with the frogs. We ask what we don't ask.
Our voices are pulleys, our words rope.
Shutterbugs of the infinite f-stop, we say what we can't see.
Zen and hubris. Rain and not a cloud in the sky.
Some make a science of the stations of the cross.
Some turn Pentecostal over the Higgs boson.
Each day circles no matter where you start.
The congregations of pollen shine equidistant in sunlit columns.
A little before twilight the wind kicks up
and ferries them off to the granaries of the invisible.

How dimly light glows from the country of the past —
and the cultured dragon seeds of one night's stories:
the apparition that rose from the drowned boy
and the mounted angel that took his soul.
Each morning leaves a trail like a slug. Dew's
silverpoint in the fresh webs. Mist like a prophet's memory.
Shy of the everlasting, what extrudes us and breaks us open?
Dark energy. Dark matter. A fine mesh.
It looks like only the smallest sparks burn through.
And if that, only for an instant. A glimmering
as one hand pinched the wicks in the kerosene lamps,
another made a rabbit out of shadow,

and then the switch clicked, the new appliances
began to hum, and we would know this in our hips.
The brilliance as the mystery diminished. Sweet electricity.

Acknowledgments

Thanks to the editors of the following publications, in which some of these poems have appeared previously, sometimes in slightly different versions:

Atlantic Monthly: "Cathedral," "Rememberer" (as "Primary Language"). *The Best American Poetry 2010:* "North Alabama Endtime." *Cave Wall:* "Lines for the Joe Wheeler Rural Electric Cooperative," "Metaphors for the Trance." *Crab Orchard Review:* "Two Quick Scenes from the Late Sixties." *Five Points:* "The Eviction," "The Moons: Notes on the Formation of Self," "North Alabama Endtime," "The Trip to Opelika." *Kenyon Review:* "The Previous Tenants," "The Art of Heaven." *New Ohio Review:* "The Ante," "Feelings, by Ashley Higgins." *New South:* "In the Days of Magical Realism," "The Elementary Principles of Rhetoric," "The Essence of Man," "The Heaven of Self-Pity." *The New Yorker:* "Hubris at Zunzal," "Starstruck." *Oxford American:* Parts of "Lines for the Joe Wheeler Rural Electric Cooperative" were first published as an essay, "A Half-Mile of Road in North Alabama." *Parnassus:* "On Criticism." *Poetry Daily:* "Deathly." *Prairie Schooner:* "Ambition," "Voice Making the Sounds of Engines." *Pushcart Prize XXXIV:* "The Eviction." *River Styx:* "The Poem of Fountains." *Shenandoah:* "In Media Res," "What Is True for a Minute." *Southern Review:* "The Competition of Prayers," "The End of Practice." *TriQuarterly:* "Deathly," "On Fiction."

"On Criticism" is for Herbert Leibowitz. "The Ante" is for James Seay. "On Fiction" is for Kent Haruf. "The Essence of Man" is for Gloria Jones. "In Media Res" is for Lee Person and Richard Russo.

Thanks to Robert Wrigley, Travis Mossotti, Allison Joseph, Amie Whittemore, Tim Shea, Jon Tribble, Edward Brunner, Leslie Adams, John Stanford-Owen, and, especially, to Dennis Sampson and Michael Collier, for reading this manuscript in earlier drafts and making suggestions.